Little Girl Lost Then Found

Bonnie Romero

Published by
Duswalt Press
280 N. Westlake Blvd Westlake Village
Suite 110
CA 91362
www.duswaltpress.com

Copyright © 2016 by Bonnie D. Romero

All rights reserved. No part of this book may be reproduced or transmitted in any form or by in any means, electronic or mechanical, including photocopying, recording, or by any information storage and retrieval system, without the written permission of the Publisher, except where permitted by law.

Manufactured in the United States of America, or in the United Kingdom when distributed elsewhere.

Romero, Bonnie
Little Girl Lost Then Found

ISBN:
Paperback: 978-1-93801539-7
eBook: 978-1-9380540-3

Cover design by: Joe Potter
Interior design: Scribe
Photo credits: supplied from author's personal collection

Contents

Chapter One: *Little Girl* — 1

Chapter Two: *Who Am I?* — 7

Chapter Three: *New Beginning* — 11

Chapter Four: *The Streets* — 15

Chapter Five: *Is This Love?* — 25

Chapter Six: *The Beginning of My End* — 35

Chapter Seven: *Playing House* — 43

Chapter Eight: *The Change* — 49

Chapter Nine: *Promises* — 55

Chapter Ten: *Realization* — 63

Chapter Eleven: *Desperate Measures* — 71

Chapter Twelve: *Finding Myself* — 77

Chapter Thirteen: *New Life* — 81

Chapter Fourteen: *Moving Forward* — 87

Dedication

First and foremost I dedicate this book to God for taking my hand and guiding me through the dark tunnel I had somehow become stuck in. Thank you for speaking to me and letting me know that everything was going to be ok and that when times were tough to just hold your hand a little tighter and we would get through it together. Because of you I know that I was put on this earth to just be myself and help others through desperate times and make people laugh with my natural silliness that I have always done.

I dedicate this book to Nicole Brown Simpson, although you are no longer here on Earth, your story helped me to become stronger and you inspired me to leave my situation before I ended up dead. I named my daughter Nicole after you, which many people did not know at the time. May you rest in peace.

I dedicate this book to my granddaughter's Audrena and Aulena and Ava, Nana Bonnie loves you and will always be there for you. Whenever you feel sad, just know that you are so special to me in my heart. Ava one day I will be able to hold you in my arms again, until then rest in peace my little Angel.

I also dedicate this book to my ex-husband who I know suffers from the disease of addiction. I will always love you and Thank you for giving me two beautiful children. Thank you for allowing me to tell my story.

Foreword

We are all here for a reason. We have meaning and purpose.
  Sometimes we don't see our gifts. To yourself you may be nothing but to others you are everything.
  Bonnie has life experience and knows how to laugh at it all.

From Desperation to Inspiration you will be
intrigued when you read the story of
Bonnie Romero

Desperation to Inspiration becoming

Bonafied

BeBonafied.com

Acknowledgements

I would like to thank my kids for being you. Each one of you is so special in every way and I am truly proud of each one of you and who you have individually become.

I would like to thank my husband for being so patient with me and always supporting my decisions, whether they be good or bad. I love you with all my heart and thank God for bringing you into my life and you asking me to dance that night.

I would like to thank my mom for allowing me to tell my story. I know it may seem hurtful and that depression is an illness that is hard to overcome, as I struggle with it from time to time myself. I love you and wouldn't want my life to be any different and I am happy that you are my mom.

Last and not least I would like to thank my Dearest Aunt Diane who was and still is my inspiration. You always loved me and stood by my side and supported me. I always wanted to make you proud. I feel your strength in me and I know in my heart you are looking down on me and you are my guardian angel. I also know in my heart that you have my Ava Marie with you under your wings waiting until we see each other again.

CHAPTER ONE

Little Girl

I was always different; I knew this since I was a little girl.

I had long, stringy blonde hair and was skinny and scrawny. I always wanted attention, demanded attention. I liked to be the center of everything.

I was the only girl growing up on our street in the small town of Kingman, Arizona. I would entertain myself with my dog Clyde, a white Samoan Husky. He was my companion and would follow me around the yard all day. I did have two stepsisters that lived in California that I had met a couple of times, but I never understood what "step" meant and I never asked.

I was always a little entertainer from as far back as I can remember. I loved to sing and I loved the feel of the microphone in my hand. I have always been somewhat of a goofball as well. I used to pee in my backyard and the neighborhood boys would come and watch me. I would excitedly tell them, "My dog Clyde will smell my pee and then pee right after me in the same spot!" It was magical to me that my dog would do that. The boys would come and watch, and it was the one time that I could get their attention, so I enjoyed having them over and laughing. I didn't realize that, boys being boys, it was because they could see my private area. I guess that was the start of my comedian ways back then and I didn't even know it.

The summers in Kingman were hot and windy and the winters were cold and dreary with snow and strong winds. I hated the cold and still do to this day.

In the summer of 1975, my dad taught me how to water-ski out on Lake Mead. I was five years old and learned very quickly—mostly out of fear. I was afraid because I couldn't see under the water; in the shallow areas I could at least see some bushes. This was around the time that the movie *Jaws* came out. I was little, so I didn't know the difference between ocean water and lake water; I was afraid that Jaws was going to get me if I was in the deep part of the lake too long. I would get up and ski until I could no longer bare it and finally let go of the ropes once my hands were numb and starting to blister. We would camp out there at Pierce Ferry every other weekend in the summer time.

My dad enjoyed camping and the lake and drinking with the rafters, as we called them, that would come in from the Grand Canyon exhibitions. Eventually we bought a boat of our own and would take the boat up river as far as we could to where the rapids would start. The furthest that I recall we went upriver was to Surprise Canyon.

In addition to my dad's boat, I had also ridden on the large gray rafts as a little girl with my dad's brother, my uncle.

They would laugh and get drunk and run off of the rafts naked when they thought the kids were asleep. My uncle had two daughters, Sherri and Angela, and I would be so happy when they would come to visit. Attention: I loved attention and craved it, and they would fight over me.

Once a summer, we had friends who would come from California in their motor home and we would camp for a week with them. I loved playing with them as well. They would tease me a lot because I was naïve but I didn't care. I just wanted someone to talk to.

Those days were some of the happiest memories of my life, my innocent days.

All the while, I was very lonely with being an only child and not having anyone to play with. I imagined that the fish in the water were my friends, and I would swim underwater a lot. I also learned to hold my breath underwater for long periods of time. I ended up with the nickname Little Mermaid because of that.

As I got older, the days at the lake became fewer and fewer, and I remember my dad drinking a lot more than before. I never really remember my parents fighting, but I do remember my mom always mad and seemed unhappy most of the time.

I never knew there was an illness called depression or for that matter bipolar disorder.

I just knew that when I would visit my friends' houses or spend the night, their lives seemed different than mine. They all ate at the dinner table together and talked about their day and played board games and enjoyed each other. At my house I had to eat at the table by myself, and I wasn't allowed to get up until my food was gone. My mom and dad would watch TV together in the living room and eat on TV trays while watching shows.

My bedtime was at 7:30 p.m. every night, which I hated because I had to go in when the streetlights came on about 6 p.m. and then eat and go to bed. I would literally sit in my bedroom and watch the kids playing outside in the street from my window.

I had a friend named Jamie who lived next door to me, and sometimes I would sneak out to talk to him from my dog Clyde's dog house. I would sit on top of it and throw small rocks at his window, and he would come to the window. I had a secret crush on him.

I had little boyfriends during school. My first little boyfriend was Mark, and then I had another boyfriend named Shayne. I thought Shayne was Indian because we lived around a lot of Indians in Arizona and he had a darker skin tone. I learned later he was Mexican.

I also had my little best friends Dawna and Gina, and for fun, we would go to the skating rink and think we were all that with our feathered hair and tight Sassoon and Sergio Valente pants.

I liked being out and about and laughing—I loved laughter—and I didn't like when it was time to go home.

I knew my dad wasn't happy, even though I was young. Kids know things and are smarter than people think they are. Later in life, my mom had said she didn't fight with him in front of me so that I wouldn't have a bad childhood. I almost wish she had, though. This way I could understand things more in life about relationships and disagreements. My mom wasn't happy either, but I never really had seen my mom smile much up to this point in life anyway.

He was working later and later, and I knew something was going to happen; I just never was prepared for what was about to happen.

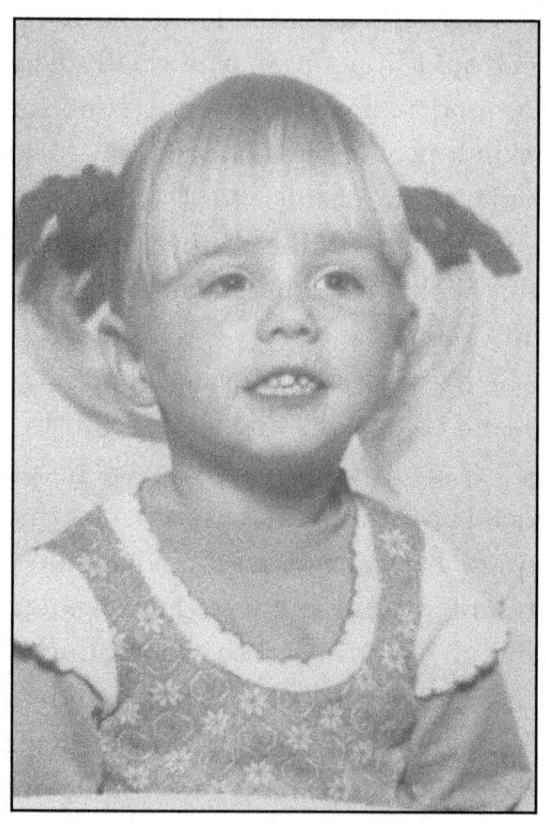

*Bonnie at five years old,
kindergarten photo*

CHAPTER TWO

Who Am I?

It was the summer of 1982; I was twelve years old. I woke up one morning to the sound of my mother crying and saw her leaning over the kitchen sink. The pain I could hear was intense, like someone had died. I asked her if there was anything that I could do to help her, and she said, "The pain I feel you cannot take away."

I knew something bad was about to happen; I just wasn't quite sure what. My father yelled from the bathroom, "Bonnie come here!" As I walked toward the bathroom, I remember his big, brown cowboy boot kicking the door open, and he looked down at me and said, "I love you," and that I could stay with him as long as I wanted.

I do not recall my dad ever telling me that he loved me before that day. Right at that moment, my mom yelled from the top of her lungs that I was not going to stay with him and that he was not my father.

This was devastating to me because I was so confused about what was going on.

If he isn't my father, then who is? Why didn't my real father want me or love me? And was my grandma who lived in Kingman, Arizona, really my grandma? Where was my grandma? My whole life as I knew it was taken from me at that moment.

I learned then that my biological father lived in Mississippi and was a severe alcoholic and homeless. I asked my mom why she didn't tell him about me, and she said she did but that he didn't want me. He couldn't take care of himself and certainly not me.

I do not remember too much about this conversation, but years later obviously it affected me more than I knew.

My mom said we were moving to California with my Aunt Diane and her friend Pat.

I had mixed emotions because I did love my Aunt Diane. She always took me to fun places and always made me feel loved and important. I thought about leaving all my friends behind, but I also thought about the beach and Disneyland.

I loved the palm trees and the damp air and so I thought, *I guess we will just give it a try.* I just didn't know how I was going to leave my dog Clyde and my friends behind who were truly all I had and everything to me at that time.

As we were preparing to move and I was saying my good-byes to everyone, including the boy next door Jamie, he and I agreed, as did Dawna, that we would not lose track of each other and that we would write each other often.

I hugged him good-bye for the last time, and I remember feeling my heart beating like I had never felt it beat before. I cried and so did he. We had never done anything like a boyfriend and girlfriend, except one time we pretended to have sex during a truth or dare game. It was innocent, though, believe it or not.

This was different though. This was a funny feeling in my stomach, like a knot, and I wanted to feel his arms tighten around me and never let go. I think we both knew it would be the last time we would see each other. I think if I had not moved when I did, something would have come out of that friendship.

My mom and I jumped in our gold Chevy pickup truck, and I turned around one last time as my mom was crying and looked at my dad's face as he stood at the gate and waved good-bye to me and then looked down. I did not yet know what had happened or why we had to move, but I could tell on my dad's face that he felt bad and almost like he was ashamed. I remember everything and every feeling I felt that day to this day.

I remember a lot from back then; I am not sure why I can but I do. Maybe I recollect it all so well because it was a traumatizing time for me. I remember every facial expression, remark, and movement.

The drive to California was the longest drive of my life. My mom sobbed the whole way.

This was the most that my mom had spoken to me my entire life. It felt good that I had her attention for a little while. It was then that she explained what had happened with my biological father and that the reason we had to leave was because my stepdad told my mom he no longer loved her.

My mother said she felt like there was another woman in the picture and that we would soon see.

I thought about all the Loretta Lynn songs that I loved, and for the first time in my life I really learned about relationships and loss and understood the country songs I'd grown up listening to.

Boy, was my world about to change in a flash.

CHAPTER THREE

New Beginning

Huntington Park, California. What a huge difference from the small dirt town of Kingman, Arizona.

Kingman had one main street, Andy Devine Boulevard, also known as "Route 66."

The most exciting thing we had to do was go to the eight cinema movie theater that had just been built up on Stockton Hill Road, or we could go to the new skating rink that was built.

If you really wanted to get crazy, Laughlin, Nevada, was about an hour away and people would go there to drink and camp. I was not old enough for all that yet.

This was so different. There were people everywhere and they mostly spoke Spanish.

I enrolled at Gage Junior High and immediately noticed that I didn't see any white people.

There were mainly Mexicans and black people, with a few Asians, and after serious searching, I found about four other white people in the entire school. This was mind-boggling to me. I wasn't used to this at all. I grew up mostly with white people before this. I had only listened to country music and soft rock, of course, and some occasional new wave because MTV had just started.

This was like a whole other world and I was a complete misfit from day one.

I never wore makeup and these girls all piled it on. And some girls had hickeys on their necks.

In the corner of the football field kids smoked cigarettes, which was allowed if you were in that area. The girls dressed very skanky if you asked me and looked like hookers from the movie *Foxes* I had seen once on TV. There were different gangs, and I remember thinking, *Why are they fighting over different blocks they live on if they are the same color.* I was so silly and naïve; I thought you were only in gangs if you had motorcycles or were different ethnic groups.

There were kids that went to school with me who lived on my block, but we were all in different classes, so we would mainly just walk together.

Bonnie Romero

I started liking Michael Jackson, Lisa Lisa and Cult Jam, Lionel Richie, DeBarge, and fast disco and funk types of music that I had never really heard before.

A few weeks after I had moved to California, I ended up receiving a letter from the boy that lived next door. He said that three days after I moved out, there was a lady at my house with long brown hair and my dad had called her by her name. He told me the name and I knew instantly who it was. It was his secretary. I remember feeling like I swallowed an apple at that moment and couldn't breathe. My first thought was, *How am I going to tell my mom*? I didn't want her to hurt more than she already did. I literally felt sick to my stomach and then I felt jealous because my dad's secretary had a daughter a little younger than me. Was my dad going to be her dad now?

I didn't have a dad and didn't know my real dad and my grandma, the only one I knew, I thought wasn't going to love me anymore either. It was a lot to take in as a young teenager.

My mother's mom, my grandma Bonnie, passed away before I was born, so I never got to meet her. My grandma Bonnie was so beautiful with blonde hair and I remember looking at pictures of her. I resembled her in a lot of ways. She had died from sclerosis of the liver from many years of drinking straight vodka. I never met my father's biological mom because she had passed away as well and I didn't know anyone on that side of my family either. I truly felt alone.

I had three distant third cousins who lived in Seattle, Washington, that I saw in the summer once a year. That was all I had.

My mom worked during the day and went to school at night. My aunt was a supervisor at that time at the El Segundo post office and worked very long hours.

I truly hung out most of the time on the streets, and this wasn't good because I was starting to lose my innocence. I babysat kids down the street and felt a family atmosphere from them. They were very good Mormon people. I went to church with them for a couple of years and loved my time with them. However, I was changing and getting mean because I was starting to get beat up at school. Life was really about to change on me now.

CHAPTER FOUR

The Streets

One day, I went to Salt Lake Park with a couple of friends from my block on Florence Avenue in Huntington Park, East Los Angeles, and we watched the people dancing.

It was intriguing to watch them break dance and pop.

I started practicing and learned fairly quickly how to dance. Around this time, I was asked to be in a dance crew called The Eclipse Girls. I agreed but did not really know what I was getting into. I had to battle against other girls and it would sometimes break out into fights. There was one girl named Maria, she was Hispanic, chubby, with long feathered hair, and wore lots of makeup, including dark brown lipstick.

Maria did not like me for whatever reason and she would constantly want to fight me.

One day I did fight her. She came up to me and started pulling my hair at the park, and we fell to the ground and basically just pulled each other's hair.

I was so afraid of her for some reason and I would try to avoid her anytime I would see her. One day she came to my front porch and rang my doorbell. She had my mom's kitten in her hands and started choking its neck until I would go outside and fight her.

I did go outside and she started pulling me by my hair and throwing me to the ground. This time I was so angry because of what she did to my mom's cat that I started punching her in the face. I actually saw I was making an impact and I started to kick her as well. We were rolling around in the wet grass of my aunt's front yard. A crowd had started to form around us.

My aunt pulled up at that time and she started yelling and threatened to call the police, so everyone started running away.

My aunt's girlfriend started yelling at my aunt that I was causing problems and that my mom and I were going to need to move soon.

I didn't like her girlfriend much. She was always mad and serious and didn't like kids.

It was around that time that I found out my aunt was gay, actually. My friends that lived on my block asked me one day if my aunt was a lesbian. I didn't know what that meant, and when I got home one night after hanging out with them, I asked her if she was a lesbian. She told me it wasn't my business and asked me where I had heard that from. I told her my friends told me that their parents had told them they couldn't come over because she was a lesbian.

A few nights later while she was smoking her normal Benson and Hedges menthol light 100s cigarettes and drinking Bacardi and Coke, she said, "Hey kid, come here. I want to talk to you." I sat on her front porch step with her and she said, "I am a lesbian. I am not proud of it. It just sort of happened and I'm going to tell you once and I never want to discuss it again." I felt bad for her because she had tears coming down her cheeks. My aunt was a very strong woman, so I knew it was upsetting for her to talk about.

She went on to tell me that my grandma Bonnie, who was her mother, would be gone a lot drinking at the bars while my grandpa was out on the sea in the navy down in San Diego, California. There was an uncle of some sort, but I do not know who.

He would molest her when she was young, and then one time when she was arrested for drunk driving, she went to jail for a while and there was a lesbian in there who had gotten a hold of her and she liked it. I guess from there on out she liked women and had a couple of girlfriends she would meet in gay bars and then met Patricia, who we called Pat. She had been with Pat for ten years at this point in our lives and she remained with her until her death at sixty-two; it was a total of thirty-two years they were together.

So that was the last time we ever discussed her sex life or choices.

At this time, I was dressing, acting, and dancing like all the sleazy girls I was hanging around in the gangs and dance clubs. A girl named Mona had taken me under her wing and she was one of the leader girls in the gang F13, better known as Florencia 13, a large Mexican gang from East L.A.

I started to wear baggy Dickie pants and net tank tops that would fall off my shoulder with tiny bras underneath. My hair was now feathered from the top of my head to my shoulders and sprayed with Aqua Net to hold the feather all day.

I started to like Mexican music even though I didn't understand it and was very fond of the Mexican group that had just come out called Menudo. This is the music group that made Latin singer Ricky Martin famous.

One day, Mona and I were hanging out after school at the little local park/police station on Miles Boulevard in Huntington Park next to our school and here came Maria again. This girl just wouldn't stop and I knew I was literally going to have to beat the hell out of her in order for her to stop bothering me. My friend Mona said in her Mexican accent to me, "Girl you better kick her ass; stick up for yourself home girl! Don't let this bitch punk you around. You have done nothing to her and she is punking you around; you show her because that's the only way she will stop. Otherwise others will punk you too if they know they can. You need to earn respect."

I knew this wasn't going to be good because I saw a crowd forming and everyone yelling, "Fight, fight."

I felt light-headed and like I was going to throw up. I walked up to her and as tough as I could be I said, "Why you walking over here by me? Get the F out of here. When you see me somewhere you do not pass me or I will drag your ass all over this park and then I will knock your teeth out and make you swallow them."

She looked at me with surprise and actually backed down. I'm pretty sure had I been by myself she would have fought me. However, Mona being with me made a big difference. She was respected in our community and people knew she was in charge of the girls in the gang. I never was jumped in, though; therefore, I never was officially in the gang.

The next Monday at school after what we called nutrition break, I was heading back to my locker but had to pass the bleachers that Maria and her friend named Stephanie were sitting on and I was all by myself.

I knew this wasn't going to be good and I said to myself, *Bonnie, don't stop. Walk by like you own this bitch*. I started to proceed and, sure enough, like I had called it in my head her friend said to me, "Hey white bitch, why don't you fight me if you think you're so tough?" I ignored her at first and kept walking because I didn't want to get in trouble again, especially not at school.

I could hear the laughter of people saying, "Eww, she called you a white bitch." I kept remembering Mona's words about not letting people punk me and especially people's respect. Although I didn't see people's faces, I just kept looking straight. I told her to shut the fuck up. I told her to meet me after school at the park and then she told me, "Make me shut up you bitch." So right then and there without thinking about consequences or anything else, I walked up to her and smashed my Tootsie Roll sucker in her face and the sticky, red candy pieces went flying everywhere. I then yelled at her, "Say one more thing to me, bitch, I'll make you swallow this whole sucker down your throat."

I turned around and started walking away toward my locker again. As I was entering the hallway of the main hall where my locker was, and the dean's office might I add, I suddenly heard the sound of rapid scuffling of feet coming at me from behind. She immediately grabbed me by the back of my head and pulled my hair and smashed my head up against the lockers. We immediately fell to the ground together and she banged my head up and down on the cold porcelain floor. I noticed the silhouettes of people's bodies and a lot of yelling going on. I grabbed her by her nose and mouth and squeezed as hard as I could while pushing her head back off of me by her throat with my right hand. I pushed her back enough that I was able to kick her off of me. I somehow ended up on top of her and banging her head into the ground while I was punching her face; I knew I was getting her good.

The teachers had come now and the fight was broken up. We were sent into the office, and as we were sitting there, she was mouthing to me that she was going to get me later and kill me. I don't know why it bothered me so much, but I didn't like to be threatened and still to this day I don't like to be threatened. I picked up the wooden desk and threw it on top of her head right there in the office. I was suspended from school for five days because of the severity of the fight and I'm sure throwing the desk on her didn't help. They were also stating that it was gang affiliated.

This actually pissed me off because it had nothing to do with gangs.

Actually, I didn't know what it had to do with for that matter. All I knew is that I was continuously in fights for no other reason than I was white. I was always grounded and fighting more and more with my mom and my aunt now as I was also starting to get rebellious. I loved freestyle music and would sneak to Elysian Park up behind Dodgers Stadium and hang out with the lowrider crews. I was actually burned out from fighting all the time and I was no longer afraid of anyone.

I was always grounded and no longer allowed to go to the park at all. It was forbidden and it was too hard to try to hide it, so I started just hanging out with the kids on my block.

A Mexican boy named Dino who lived down the street from me had a cousin named Abraham and he was a popper/break-dancer. He was cute and asked me to be his girlfriend. We started going out but I was only thirteen. So what all are we actually going to do, right? I really liked him and he asked me to kiss him after a few days together. I literally ran into the bathroom and squirted toothpaste into my mouth because I was afraid my mouth would be dirty. When he kissed me for the first time, he started laughing because he said my mouth taste like a tube of toothpaste and I laughed because he was right. It broke the ice and I remember from that day on I loved to kiss. He was not into gangs and was always dressed nice and smelled good. I remember even today how much he broke my heart when he broke up with me because I wouldn't go further with him. There was another girl in a dance crew and he broke up with me to be with her. I cried and cried and remember it felt like the end of the world. Yes, my first little break up.

*Bonnie at seven years old,
at Lake Mead*

CHAPTER FIVE

Is This Love?

I soon met a boy named Frankie that lived in Alhambra but would come visit his cousin Erick who lived a block before mine. I met them through a girl named Raquel who I went to school with and walked with. She had two brothers named Carlos and Johnny.

Frankie asked me to be his girlfriend and I liked the way he dressed with Le Tigre shirts in baby blue and blush pink and Levi jeans and Vans tennis shoes. He was more into rock music and liked Mötley Crüe. He was faster than Abraham was and I could tell he had been around with the girls. He wouldn't ask me to kiss; he would just grab me and pull me in and kiss me. He was a bit rough though and bossy and I kind of didn't like it. His kisses were sloppy and I felt like a dog had lapped me with his tongue every time he would finish kissing me.

It scared me that he was rough and then he told me I was his and that he was going to crucify me. I didn't know what that meant and didn't want to know. He lived too far away and I didn't like the way he was only available and around when he wanted to be. He also got me in trouble. One day, he told me to give him hickeys, so I did.

I gave him big ones all around his entire neck. He looked like he had a disease when I was done with him. I sat on his lap facing him and sucked every part of his neck while listening to Michael Jackson singing "Pretty Young Thing" and "Billie Jean." I was in my friend's garage on a recliner and his mom came and picked him up shortly after. She must not have seen the hickeys at that moment. About a half hour later, she came driving back up to the garage where we were listening to music and got out screaming that I was a whore and asking what did I do to her son's neck. It's kind of funny when I think back because I remember he was sixteen years old and I was only thirteen years old. I truly didn't want to give them to him but he kept telling me to. I know I knew better but he surely knew better than I. She then said I better tell my mom myself because she was going to tell her the next day. I remember Frankie just sitting in the car and not even looking at me while she was yelling at me and he was eating a white powder donut. I don't like powder donuts to this day because of that. I did tell my mom and I ended up grounded for two weeks.

I broke up with him after that.

His cousin Johnny who lived there with his cousin Erick and I had become very close in the meantime. I remember he made me laugh and was so good to me.

He had the cutest smile and the brightest, pretty white perfect teeth and wavy black hair. He was shorter than me though and I remember that I didn't like that. His height was the only thing I could think of that I didn't like about him.

I knew they were Puerto Rican and his mom Vicky was beautiful and danced salsa. I remember that I wanted to learn to dance like that.

I did like him and we did kiss one day shortly after I broke up with his cousin and I remember feeling so bad for liking him since I had dated with his cousin. We would walk around the block and he was actually making me forget about the gangs and the lowriders' ways. He also liked hard rock but he did know how to break dance and liked that music too. He was more mature though and would go to school and also worked.

I remember that his dad lived in Mexico and he was the oldest in the home and helped his mom.

One day shortly after, we were making out and I had gotten farther with him than I had the other boys. He would kiss me so softly and sensually. He knew just how to hold my hair. He would pull it from the back of my head while kissing my neck and it would give me chills up and down my body. He was very passionate and I wanted him. I loved kissing him and the way he held me tight and I felt like everything was OK. I hated when it was time for him to leave or for me to leave because we had a connection.

He said to me one night after going out for a couple of weeks, "Let me make love to you."

I said, "Yes I want to, but how are we going to do this?" Keep in mind, I was thirteen and he was fifteen years old.

"You can stay at my cousin's house and say you're staying with Raquel and then no one will know. In the middle of the night, you come and be with me when everyone is sleeping," he said. I agreed and we planned it for that weekend.

My friend Raquel knew I was seeing her brother even though we hid it from others and acted like we were just friends since I was actually his cousin Frankie's ex-girlfriend.

I didn't want to use her though to have the benefit of being with her brother. I spent most of the evening that

Friday night with her as I would coyly and flirtatiously look at Johnny and he would meet my eyes.

That night was cold and I remember the house was quiet as I kept waiting for everyone to go to sleep. His cousin Erick always had girls in and out of his room. I could hear his girlfriend and him having sex and their bed hitting the wall. This just made me even more want to go have sex with Johnny as soon as I had the chance. I figured I would go now because everyone was asleep and Erick was busy with his girlfriend. I sneaked quietly into the living room where Johnny was sleeping on a foam bed and blankets. I went and got under the blanket with him. I loved feeling his chest by mine and we started to kiss slowly and passionately. He was kissing me on my breasts and touching me all over my body and slipped his hand down into my panties and I remember wanting him to touch me more and more.

We started breathing heavily and I turned and got on top of him and was kissing him. I could feel his erect penis on me rubbing back and forth and I was now ready for him to enter me. I remember thinking, *Oh boy, this is it.*

I had no protection and I was not on birth control. But I didn't care.

The kitchen lights suddenly turned on and it was his cousin Erick walking up to the sink to get water. He pours water in a cup, takes a drink, and looks over at us. I'm covered but on top of Johnny trying to not move and pretend to be asleep.

Erick asked, "What are you guys doing?" He told me to get up, and I said, "I need to dress. Part of my clothes are off." He said, "I can't believe you are with Johnny and you were just with Frankie." Johnny told him to shut up and mind his own business. He said, "No you guys are too young." And I remember Johnny being upset and telling him, "You are eighteen, so shut the hell up."

You can imagine the embarrassment I felt over this, and I also felt like a complete whore.

We didn't try to do this again because we were afraid of getting caught and decided we would try again when the time was right.

It was soon approaching a Christmas dance at school and Johnny couldn't go because he was in high school. I was in eighth grade and wouldn't be in ninth grade like him until a few more months. Johnny and I were hardly able to see each other because of the different schools and homework and life.

I was walking home by myself one day and I met a guy named Albert, but he told me to call him Beto. Albert was Mexican and the same height as me at five foot three, and he was dressed like a gangster. He was waiting at the bus stop to take the RTD bus to Bell

Gardens, which was about fifteen minutes east from where I lived. He asked me if I needed a companion to walk me home and I said, "No, I'm OK."

He said, "OK, well if you ever do, pretty girl, just let me know."

I said, "OK, thanks Beto."

As I walked home, I thought to myself that was rather blunt of him, but also I was kind of flattered that he called me pretty girl and acted interested in actually walking me home.

The next day was the Christmas dance at school and it was on Friday, December 21st, and I know this to this day because I remember it was three days after my birthday. It was the beginning of the rest of my life as I would know it.

I went to the dance with a couple of my friends and standing right where you purchase the tickets was Beto. He asked me if I had $3 so that he could buy a ticket to get into the dance because he lost his money. I gave him $5 so that he could buy a ticket and a cookie and a fruit punch inside.

I carried along with my friends and dancing to Michael Jackson's "Wanna Be Starting Something," and Madonna's "Holiday," and Adam Ant, and Boy George's

"Karma Chameleon." Beto came up on the dance floor and started dancing with me, and then we went to go get a cookie and a punch. As we stood up against the wall and ate, he pulled me toward him and said, "I want to kiss you."

I said, "No, I have a boyfriend."

And he said, "I don't care." He kissed me and played with a hole in the pocket of my tight, white-colored striped pants with zippers on the bottoms. My friends were annoyed and didn't like him. I don't blame them now, but at that time I wasn't thinking.

"Careless Whisper" by Wham came up and we danced to it on the dance floor. He had charisma and was very funny. He would make me laugh and a lot of girls liked him and wanted to be with him. This made me want him for some reason.

Wouldn't you know it; Maria and her friend Monique liked him.

You know, after I found out Maria liked him and I could rub it in her face that he liked me, I was going to make sure she saw me talking to him, dancing with him, and whatever I wanted with him. This was a game now and I was going to win.

I have always wondered what my life would be like now had I looked the other way.

I left the dance that night and said good-bye, not thinking too much of it. It was Christmas break until the following week. I didn't really see Johnny much, but when I did, I told him that I thought we needed some time apart. He said we have enough time apart. I knew about a girl named Pilar who I had heard he was seeing at high school. She was Puerto Rican and short like him and petite. He was mad at me. He said I was looking for excuses to be single and if I wanted to break up just to say it.

He was right and I know all this now. I was looking for an excuse.

When school started up again that first Monday after school, Johnny ended up waiting for me at the park next to my school and we bought french fries. While we were eating them, Beto walked up to us and asked Johnny for a cigarette. Johnny told him, "I don't have any cigarettes and if I did I wouldn't give you one. Why don't you go fuck yourself and stop talking to my girlfriend. I know about you."

They started fighting and I didn't know what to do. Technically, Johnny never actually asked me to be his girlfriend, but I also had kind of grown apart from him and I knew that he was also interested in that girl, Pilar. I kind of liked the bad boy in Beto and, of course, the gangster way.

The fight got broken up and I remember that I found myself leaning more toward Beto than Johnny. Johnny told me good-bye that day and didn't really talk to me much after that. This is definitely one person in my life that I wish I could find and apologize for hurting him. I feel like I deserved every bit of sorrow about to come when they say "what comes around goes around." I looked him up on Facebook years later and every social media outlet over the years and I never could find him.

My life changed after this day; it was the ending of innocence and beginning of unhappiness for me from that day forward.

CHAPTER SIX

The Beginning of My End

I soon started calling Beto by his actual name, Albert, because I didn't like Beto. I didn't like the sound of it. Plus, I noticed that his family called him Albert and only bad friends called him Beto.

Albert was a charmer; somehow he could make me feel like I was the prettiest girl in the world.

It had only been about a week when instead of him walking me home, we took the bus to his house so that I could meet his family. As we approached his front porch, I noticed a small Mexican lady slouched over in a chair on the porch holding a Budweiser can.

She was almost passed out and he was embarrassed by her. I knew she was drunk. I could tell by her slurred speech. She seemed sad to me and had tears coming down her face.

This was my first encounter with the dysfunction I was going to endure. Albert had a large family. He was the baby and he was fourteen years old.

His mother had a total of thirteen kids. Out of the thirteen kids, there were two sets of fraternal twins. His mother was an alcoholic, and I think she was done parenting by the time she had Albert. I can't blame her; she was probably worn out.

I met his siblings and they all seemed very loving and funny. They were playing dominoes. I never knew how to play but liked watching them. I had never learned because I never had anyone to play games with.

I liked the family environment. They all would talk to me and listen to my stories, and I loved having them listen to me and laugh over my foolishness.

Albert and I were talking in his sister's car in the driveway and I was telling him I needed to go home it was getting late. We were kissing and he said the words, "I want to make love to you." Those words that I would always hear from my past boyfriends and then something would happen and we would break up.

I thought, *I'm not going to let this night end and not fulfill it.*

Why I thought this, I guess I will never know. I was so young and I look back now and think I was crazy! I didn't feel young, though. I felt like I was older.

That very night we went to his bedroom, which was the converted garage. It was very cold and basically only consisted of an electric heater, a bed, a dresser, and a stereo that sat on the dresser.

We were listening to love songs on Kost 103 FM and the group Chicago came on. "You're The Inspiration" and "Hard Habit to Break" came on and we started making out.

I actually was the one that moved his hands onto my breasts and I loved the way he caressed them so softly. He was a lousy kisser; he didn't kiss me like Johnny did, but hell, I didn't care at this point. He moved his hands down into my pants and they were tight, so I undid my zipper and pulled them off.

He started touching me between my legs and I was trembling. I remember thinking, *I need to stop*. But I couldn't stop and I didn't want him to either.

I will just let him get a little further, enough that he will stay with me and not leave me.

I was embarrassed for him to see my body from the light of the stereo. I had small breasts. He rubbed his cheeks over them back and forth and told me how beautiful my body was and how lucky he was to be with me.

He then kissed down my stomach and started kissing me between my legs. I never knew of this feeling and I remember feeling like I was shaking with so much pleasure and couldn't believe I was doing that. It seemed so dirty and I felt like I was doing the forbidden. I didn't care at this moment; I didn't care about anything. I just wanted to be with him. He came up and entered me. I remember an excruciating pain that shot through my body. I told him to stop and go slow. He said, "You are a virgin?"

And I said, "Yes."

He smiled the most romantic and adoring smile and said, "Oh Bonnie, you are mine now forever." I believed this and thought it would be forever. I wanted to be with him forever. I wanted to be a part of his family. I knew it right then and there.

After cleaning up and heading home that night, I got home and my mom had called the police. She said, "I know you were with that boy Albert and I don't like him."

I said, "I like him and I didn't do anything wrong for you to call the police."

My mom said, "Bonnie, there is something about him, something in his face and eyes that I know he is no good for you." I was grounded for being home late, so I would ditch school so I could see him.

All I thought about was Albert. My grades were falling and I wanted to be with him every second of my day. He loved me and I loved him.

Shortly afterward, things started to change; he would follow me if I was with my friends. He would randomly just pop up.

I was in class one day and I was speaking with a fellow male student about an assignment. When I was let out of class, Albert asked me what I was talking to him about.

"We were discussing homework, that was all," I said. He pulled his hand back and smacked me as hard as he could across my face and said to me that he better not ever catch me talking to a guy again. My face immediately started to burn and turn red. I started crying and the teacher came out and asked what was going on.

We walked away and he was hugging me and said I was upset about something but I was OK. This was the first time he had hit me. He told me how sorry he was, and he promised me it would be the last time he ever would. He said he smacked me because he just got jealous and the thought of losing me, who was so beautiful, scared him and he lost control. I believed him and actually took that as a compliment. Somehow or another, it ended up twisted around and I found myself saying sorry to him.

From this point forward, I little by little became Albert's girl. I wasn't allowed to have friends and I wasn't allowed to look toward a guy or make eye contact. If I did, it was for sure a smack and/or he would pull my hair. I don't know why I didn't stick up for myself. I didn't fight back because somehow or another it was always my fault. If I just wouldn't upset him and do as he said, then that wouldn't happen.

He actually had convinced me of this and would always say sorry after and then love me and buy me things, and it would be OK. I even sometimes liked to fight with him because I looked forward to the making up phase that would follow after.

I was totally submissive to him and in a totally dysfunctional relationship; I didn't even know it. I would watch romance movies and wish I had that. He told me it's like that only in the movies and I believed him.

My mom and aunt hated him, and my friends that did still talk to me hated him as well. They would tell me they saw him with a girl here or there and he would deny it.

He said they were just jealous of our relationship and now I was no longer allowed to talk to them because they would fill my head up with lies and cause problems for us.

My mom and aunt decided that come summer break we were moving to Culver City, which was about forty miles from Huntington Park where I lived. It was also closer to work for my mom because she worked at Hughes Helicopters, which then became McDonnel Douglas and then was bought out by Boeing.

I didn't want to move and have to start over again. I wanted to stay there with him forever.

Bonnie's senior photo

CHAPTER SEVEN

Playing House

Culver City High School was full of snobby rich kids and all nationalities.

The school was predominately white, Mexican, and black.

This was a whole other class than what I had been around for the last couple of years over in East L.A.

I went to school with a lot of child actors and I lived on Sepulveda Boulevard, only two miles from MGM Studios, which later had become Paramount Studios.

I couldn't wait to get home after school each day and wait for Albert's phone call.

He would call me to make sure I got home OK each day. Oh, he loved me so much, right?

Now I know this was just a control tactic to see what I was up to and make sure I wasn't out with friends.

I literally was missing an average of probably a week of school every month. I would write my own sick notes. The school had my signature on file, so I would always get away with it. Until one day I thought, *I better throw them off*, and wrote a note that I had pink eye. I didn't know that you were supposed to have a doctor's excuse to get back in school. I finally got caught and remember my mom had my absence slips spread all over the counter in the administrative office and was so angry. She said, "Bonnie, you write my name so well that I wouldn't know my signature from yours other than the fact that I haven't written any this year."

I had a total of twenty-eight excuse slips in front of me and she grabbed me by my ear and twisted it. She said, "I know this is Albert's doing." She then said I was no longer able to see him ever again and that it was forbidden.

I still sneaked to see him by taking the RTD Bus #108 to see him at least once a week and he would come see me on weekends and we would go hang out at Venice Beach.

Around this time, I was in my senior year in high school and Albert and I had been together for three years and the housing market was booming in the San Bernardino area and Fontana.

Albert's brothers were all in their own construction business and offered him a job doing various construction tasks from painting to roofing.

He was getting paid $8.00 per hour, which was really good then considering minimum wage was $3.35.

I had obtained my first job at the Taco Bell directly across the street from me.

It was perfect and I got to see a lot of celebrities while working there.

I saw Magic Johnson with many women, especially blonde, white women that looked like cheerleaders. I knew his wife was a black lady named Cookie because I read *The Enquirer* and he was always in the headlines. He had a light yellow Mercedes and it was awkward to see him in the drive-thru all the time because we knew he was cheating. A few years later, we heard about him having AIDS.

Another regular was Gary Coleman who was Arnold on the show *Different Strokes*. Gary was very short and dark. I remember he always had different vehicles and always sat on big books. He sounded like a woman in the speaker each time he placed an order in the drive-thru. He asked me out a few times and wanted to take me to Switzerland for companionship while shooting a movie of some sort. He was actually a lonely man.

I really loved talking with all the different people while working there and loved helping people from then forward.

I also met Holly Robinson while she was filming *21 Jump Street* and *Howard the Duck*. She was a very nice, down-to-earth, beautiful woman and was so kind and let me sit down with her for a soda when I asked her for her autograph.

I also met Leonardo DiCaprio when he was still a child, at Hard Rock Restaurant in L.A. He was just a little boy and not heard of yet and I remember then thinking he will be someone one day.

Around this time in high school, there was a guy that was interested in me named James. He was half-Mexican and half-Hawaiian.

He worked out all the time and had nice muscles and a nice Chevy Camaro. I wish so badly I had given him a chance.

He even came to my apartment one time with flowers to ask me out on a date.

I hid from him, though, and avoided him. Eventually, he graduated and moved on with his life.

Time was moving on, and so was Albert apparently, because I started hearing about different girls he was cheating on me with. One in particular was named Donna.

I ended up confronting him about her and he told me that he was lonely and needed someone by his side to take care of him. He gave me the ultimatum to move to Fontana with him or we would have to break up because he couldn't live like that anymore.

I was fighting with my mom constantly because of Albert and I really was in love, so I decided to run away. It would be easier to ask for forgiveness than permission.

I didn't realize it at the time but this was another tactic of his to control me and have his way.

I was excited about moving with him and thought I would just finish school in Fontana, but I didn't realize that I had to have my mom's permission since I was a minor.

My mom refused to allow me to go to school there, thinking it would cause me to move back home. I never moved back home, so I didn't finish school at that time.

My home was with Albert, and he loved me and I loved him.

I was a good homemaker and made Albert breakfast burritos in the morning and sandwiches for lunch and then a big dinner each night. It was also my duty to make sure and have his bath ready each night after dinner and wash his back for him and then give him clean clothes to change into. I actually was proud to do this.

Around this time, I started noticing that each morning he would take a pill that he said helped him stay awake. I didn't think much of it at this point. I thought that was pretty cool that he could work all day and still be energetic when he got home.

He started to get home later and later at times, and I would hear about girls Albert talked to after work when they would stop for a drink from his brothers. But I thought it was all lies.

I started getting bored and wanted to do something with my life, but I wasn't sure of what I wanted to do. Plus my life revolved around Albert. He knew I wanted to work. Shortly there afterward, I found out that I was pregnant.

CHAPTER EIGHT

The Change

I was eighteen years old when I found out I was pregnant and thought, *What in the hell am I going to do?* I was already nine weeks pregnant when it was confirmed. I was scared to death because I knew my mom would be pissed and I really didn't want to hurt her or my aunt. I knew they would make me get an abortion, so I didn't tell them I was pregnant until I was almost six months along.

I never knew whether I was having a boy or a girl because back in the eighties you had to pay about $750 to find out the sex, and it was done by abstracting amniotic fluid. They were not as high tech as they are now with ultrasounds. We didn't have a lot of money.

My pregnancy took a toll on me, and I gained 53 pounds. I was 108 pounds when I became pregnant and I was 163 pounds the day before I delivered.

Albert started acting really strange. I thought it was because I was pregnant but I wasn't sure because it seemed like it happened when he would take "that pill."

I do have to say that during my pregnancy with my son, Daniel, Albert was very supportive; he always bought me whatever I was craving and doted on me. Those were the best times we had together.

In December 1989, my son Daniel was born and I was in so much bliss. I looked down at my Daniel and knew I would love him always, I made him a song that was just his; I loved to sing to him and he would quiet down from fussing whenever he would hear me sing.

All my happiness would come to an abrupt end within a few months. We lived by ourselves now and Albert couldn't keep a job. He was no longer taking the pills but snorting them through his nose and I found out it was called "speed," known today as meth.

He started staying out at night more and more, and when I would say something, it would become a fight. I didn't know what to do. I had let myself go and continued to gain weight after my pregnancy and didn't really care about fixing myself up. I decided to go back to night school and get my degree in finances. I signed up for banking occupation classes at Regional Occupation Center in Redlands, California.

I liked being around people again and talking and laughing and sharing goofy stories of my day with all my fellow classmates. I knew my calling was to be around people, groups of people. I did not like being alone and quiet.

The jealousy started in from Albert at this point, as he didn't want me having friends and wanted me to be sheltered by him. I know now this was a dysfunctional way to keep me under his wing.

One night when he came and picked me up from night school, he was high and I knew that meant that we didn't have any money. He would use the money from his paychecks to buy his drugs and then be awake for a few days. He was sweating profusely and smelled weird; I asked him why he went and got high especially when he had our son in the car with him. He told me not to worry about it and that he saw me talking to a guy. He would make stuff up all the time to create fights with me.

I told him, "You did not and you are lying." When we got back to the house, I put my son to sleep and went to bed. He came in the room and started pulling my pajama pants off of me and then pulled my panties off and started smelling them.

I didn't know what to think about this and had not ever seen him crazy like this.

He started touching me and rubbing me between my legs and then began to perform oral sex on me that seemed like it lasted for hours.

I always knew that anytime he was high it meant that we would end up having sex and it would last forever because it would take him forever to finally finish.

I have to admit that those times were the best sex we would have. This is why I would be mad, but then at the same time, I knew it would be erotic and hot sex that night. I know it sounds crazy, but this is true. He was a very good lover and loved to please. He definitely knew how to please a woman and was well endowed as well.

We ended up having to move because he couldn't keep a job and we had no money. We ended up moving to a house in San Bernardino and I thought things would get better. Things did not get better because we moved even closer to where he got his drugs and he was now doing cocaine and speed and also drinking.

I hid things from my family more and more because I did not want them to know what I was going through. I was embarrassed and also didn't want to hear "I told you so."

I was going to change him; one way or another I was going to get him off the drugs.

He was not coming home sometimes at night. I was very lonely.

I was still taking classes and one night he picked me up and asked me who some guy in my class was. I did not know and he smacked me.

He smacked me across my face and busted my lip. I got mad and smacked him back across his face. This infuriated him, so he picked me up and threw me down on the kitchen floor and started slamming my head up and down on the hard laminate. Then he started choking me until I felt like my head was going to blow off of my body and my eyes felt like they were bulging out of my head. He was yelling at me to never hit him again and that he was teaching me a lesson. I was crying and lifted my shaking hand up at him and he grabbed my hand and bit my fingers and then turned around and went out the front door. The car sped off in the driveway and I heard him crash into something down the street. I ran outside and he had taken off. I still don't know what he hit, but I ended up with a huge dent on the front end of the car.

This really scared me because I had never seen him that crazy before. Now I was sitting there crying and shaking. My son was approaching one and a half years old now. He was screaming because he had witnessed all that. Even as little as he was, I know he knew it was bad.

I then instantly felt bad because I felt like if I just hadn't smacked him back this would have never happened. Why didn't I just shut my mouth and let him hit me and be done with it?

I was worried about him because we didn't have cell phones back then and I had no way to communicate with him. I was also so angry because I didn't know where he was and I just couldn't understand any of this. I didn't do anything wrong for God's sake.

When he came back home I was asleep. I woke in the morning and found my school books all ripped up with pages missing. He had gotten some sort of a crayon and had colored over the pages saying he was looking for codes. I didn't know what he was talking about. He took me outside and said there were people in the trees watching us and that the government was after him.

This was the crazy stuff that I dealt with for the next few years.

CHAPTER NINE

Promises

There comes a time in all our lives when we either change our situations or we accept it and live the same day to day.

I knew I had to do something, but at this point I feared Albert. I wanted to leave. I no longer felt like our relationship was a marriage and I was not happy. I watched a lot of love stories on TV and would fantasize about having someone love me. I didn't want to be married to him anymore. I had tried to leave a couple of times and he would threaten to kill me.

I was so lonely and Albert was cheating on me with different girls all the time.

He was always with girls that wanted drugs; he would give them drugs, and they would pay him with sex and money.

There was one night he came home and had two girls with him. He had a blonde and a Mexican girl with him and he said he had business to handle. I will admit, at this point I didn't care that it was illegal because at least we would have electricity paid for the month.

He told me to go to our room and not come out until he came and let me out. So I went to our bedroom and I took my son with me who was now almost three years old. We started playing video games and I turned the volume up loud so that we couldn't hear anything going on outside the room.

I put my head against the door and heard him talking to the girls, and then all of a sudden it was completely silent. I was standing at the door for the longest time wondering what was happening in the living room. I had to use the bathroom and thought to myself, *This is my house and if I want to use the bathroom then I can, damn it!*

I told my son to stay in the room and don't come out and that I will be right back.

I quietly opened the door and looked around the hallway door into the living room. I saw lines of powder on the coffee table and a muted porn playing on the TV and Albert was sitting on the couch with his legs open. The Mexican girl was giving him a blow job on her knees and the blonde girl was sitting on his face looking down on the other girl and rubbing his chest with her hands. I couldn't believe what I was seeing. I felt mixed emotions, as it took my breath away to actually witness my husband having a threesome.

My heart was pounding in my chest so loud I thought he could hear it.

The pit of my stomach felt like someone had punched me, and at the same time I was turned on by witnessing this, as crazy as it sounds.

I must have gasped or made a noise or something because at that very moment he jumped up and threw them off of him and came running at me and told me, "What did I tell you about coming out of the room?" I told him I had to use the bathroom and he grabbed a cane that was up against the wall and he hit me on the back of my head with it I want to say three times. I'm not sure because it knocked me out. I remember waking up on the hallway floor and my son was crying, "NO, Daddy, NO! Don't hurt my mommy!" This broke my heart because I never wanted him to see this or endure this.

I had enough and I went to sit up. I was dizzy and the room was spinning. There was a huge bump on the back of my head like a baseball. I touched the lump and it squished in and out; I still to this day have an indention on the back of my head from that. Albert yelled at the girls to leave and not come back. They left, and he went to get an icepack and put it on the back of my head. He held me in his arms on the floor while he rocked me and told he was sorry and that he loved me and this would never happen again. He helped me up and changed my clothes, as I had somehow in the middle of all this peed in my pants.

He promised me he was going to change and asked me to give him a chance because he loved me and our family and wanted to make things right. I told him I was going to forgive him but he needed to mean it.

It was about two weeks later when he didn't come again one night. I knew he was going to come home high because that was the only time that he would be out all night. I was waiting up for him and was eating a cup-of-noodles soup on the couch and started to fall asleep while watching *Robin Hood*.

I looked and noticed the blinds started to move; a man's foot and leg come through the front window of the house. I yelled that he better go away because my husband was in the back room and will shoot him. He laughed and said, "I know you're home alone, bitch, so shut the fuck up." I got up and started screaming and ran toward him with my fork I was eating with earlier. He ended up going back out the window and ran off down the street. It was so weird and random and really scared the shit out of me.

I got on my house phone and called Albert's brothers and sister's houses to see if anyone had seen Albert and to tell him to come home and what happened.

It was about midnight now and I heard someone knocking on the backdoor very lightly. I went back and looked though the blinds and saw it was my brother-in-law.

I liked him a lot because I always got along with him and could talk to him.

He said that he heard what had happened and came to check on me because he was worried about me and Albert was high and out on the town.

I asked him why he came in the back door instead of the front door and he said in case the guy came back he would catch him off guard. He told me that he had parked a block away also.

He sat across from me on one couch and I was on the other couch. I was crying and told him I was so tired of living like this and wanted to show my son a better life. I told him I wanted to work and have friends again and about how sad and lonely I was. He told me he didn't like the way his brother treated me and I didn't deserve that.

He told me I needed to leave and teach his brother a lesson so that he will see I am not playing around and maybe that will make him change. I said, "No, it will make things worse because anytime I threaten to leave he tells me he will kill me and no one will find me."

Right then, the front door was kicked in and Albert yelled, "AHA! I caught you." I jumped, as this scared me. I said, "Caught me what?" Albert then looked at his brother and said, "You are really fucked up to be fucking around with my old lady." His brother then said, "I am not fucking around with your old lady, bro, but let me tell you something, Albert.

"If you don't take care of her and love her the way she deserves, she will find somebody and she will leave you and it is going to be your fault for not taking care of your wife!" His brother turned around and looked at me and said, "Well you are safe now, Albert's home, but remember what I said."

Then he left. I knew he was right. I hated to admit it. But I knew he was right.

Albert grabbed me by my arm and put a gun to my head and said, "Bitch, get in the car." He was sweating and he was drunk. I could tell he was on an extreme amount of drugs and he had been up for days. My son was sleeping in his bed in his room and he told me to leave him there. I said, "No, please let me take him with us."

Albert said, "No, he needs to stay because we will be right back."

He drove off fast and erratic all the while with one hand on the wheel and the other hand holding the gun pointed at my head. I was crying and said, "Please what are you doing? I haven't done anything. Please, Albert, take me home."

He said, "I am going to shoot you and throw your body in Lytle Creek in Fontana and no one will find you. And when they do, the animals will have eaten most of you." I saw the craziness in his eyes and I knew he was serious. I knew it was true because he made me leave my son alone at home!

My heart was pounding and I could see his mouth moving, as he was still talking but my ears had gone deaf because I was in so much fear. I don't think I have ever feared anything again like I did that night.

We were coming up on a red light and I felt a screwdriver on the side of the passenger seat I was sitting in. I thought in my mind that I will stab him and jump out and possibly save my life.

I got it and pulled it up and went to hit him in the temple with it but somehow missed. I jumped out and started running and screaming. A car behind us stopped and three cholo guys asked me what was going on. I said, "He is going to kill me."

They said, "We will see about that." They started walking really fast toward Albert and our car.

Albert got out and told them, "Hey man, I just caught my old lady in bed with my best friend." This was a complete lie and I don't even know why he said that.

They looked at me and looked at him and he told them, "I'm just going to smack her around a little bit and scare her and that's it man, she isn't worth killing."

They said, "OK cool, bro, just take it easy, man, life in the pen sucks, man. Chill out."

This really was a reality check for me because I know he was going to kill me that day. I saw it in his eyes and couldn't believe that he could that easily make up a lie to justify his actions.

I knew then I needed out and quick. No more promises.

CHAPTER TEN

Realization

Shortly afterward, O. J. Simpson allegedly killed Nicole Brown Simpson. I watched that whole trial and thought, *That could be me.* I felt so bad for her because I knew the pain she felt and probably how much she tried to make her marriage work just to be killed once she left him.

That story intrigued me and I was starting to figure ways to leave Albert for good.

I immediately packed up bags of my clothes and called my brother-in-law to take me to my sister-in-law's so I could stay with her.

He came and picked me up, but said if I stayed there he would not be learning his lesson and that I needed to go somewhere he couldn't find me.

I checked into a Motel 6 and he paid for me to be there for a couple of days.

My brother-in-law walked me to my room and sat on the bed next to me and looked at me in my eyes and said, "I am so sorry you're going through this, I wish I had met you first and wasn't in a relationship and you married to my brother." This made me feel uncomfortable because he was my brother-in-law. I was also uncomfortable because of the whole situation with the night of him coming to check on me and I could see how that looked suspicious to Albert, no matter how innocent it was.

He held my hand and pulled my face toward his with his other hand and kissed me on my lips. I felt a passion in my body I had not felt for many years with Albert.

I wanted to stop him from kissing me because I knew it was wrong. But he kissed me so softly and passionately that I couldn't stop him. I felt loved and special and warm inside. I knew he needed to leave right then and there because I was very vulnerable and I knew I wanted and needed his touch and caresses that I had not felt for so long. I also loved his ex-wife very much and was good friends with her. I instantly thought of how this would impact everyone in our family and I didn't want to hurt anyone. I also didn't want to be a whore. I asked him to leave. He left and I sat there alone again. I had a smile on my face as I felt attention and wanted.

I lie in the bed in that dark, cold room and then felt ugly inside and like such a horrible person.

The phone kept ringing in the room and no one would answer. This freaked me out. I thought it was Albert. I had a flashback to when I was dating Frankie during my younger teenage years and then his cousin Johnny and thought, *What in the fuck is wrong with me? Why do I have to mess around with family? This is so wrong.*

I grabbed my son from his sleep and called a cab, which picked us up and took us to my sister-in-law's house. I was scared and felt so shameful. When I arrived to her house, her teenage son opened the door and had to actually pay my cab fare. My sister-in-law took me back home the next day in her car and on the drive there was complete silence. I felt so guilty and at this point was having an emotional affair with my brother-in-law although we never had sex. However, I wanted him to hold me and love me and continue to say all would be OK.

No one ever knew this because I felt so scared for Albert to ever know. I was sure that he would kill me and probably kill his brother if he ever found out. I felt guilty, so I tried to make things work once again with Albert for a while. But it was over and I knew in my heart it was over. He loved the drugs and women more than any high I could give him.

I decided to take control back in my life; I told Albert he needed to change and that I was truly going to leave and honestly didn't care if he killed me because I was going to kill myself first and he wouldn't have a chance.

I also asked my brother-in-law to not contact me anymore.

I started taking counseling classes at college because I wanted to be a drug counselor.

Albert was trying to get off the drugs but just couldn't do it. He was going back and forth to jail for traffic tickets and minor stuff.

Each time that he went to jail, I got a little stronger, as he was losing his control over me.

I got a job at a check cashing place and I loved it, especially making $5.40 per hour. The check cashing place was my favorite job that I had and I wanted to work as a bank teller to work my way up to branch manager one day.

One night, I had to close the store I worked at and Albert waited for me in the car outside and a customer was having me wire money to Zacatecas, Mexico.

It took longer than usual because the fax lines were backed up.

When I closed and came outside, he yelled at the customer in Spanish. I didn't know what he said to him, but the guy got in his car shaking his head and just looked at me. I was so embarrassed and asked Albert why he yelled at him. Albert grabbed me by my hair and pulled me by my ear and said, "You think you're cool, bitch? I know what you're up to and you think you're going to get away with cheating on me?"

I told him, "Albert, I am not cheating on you. This is what I'm talking about, you get crazy and I can't handle it and you are starting a fight with me over nothing. I'm not doing anything and I just want to go home. I have to open the store in the morning."

He spit on my face and grabbed it with his hand the way he always would, pulling my head down by my hair, and smashed my face into the asphalt on the ground by the car. He turned my head back and forth so that my face was being scratched up. I lifted myself up with rocks still stuck on my cheek, my face burning from road rash, and got in the car so there would be no noticeable scene outside of my work. I tried not to cry and show weakness. It was pure silence in the car that night, other than the sounds of my tears as they streamed down my face. My face was hot and pulsing and throbbing.

I hated him more and more and despised the thought of him even touching me as I went to sleep that night.

The next day it was time to go to work and I noticed Albert was gone when I woke up.

I had bought a new outfit and put it on to wear to work that day. I was so happy to have bought it with my own money. I didn't have many clothes and the other girls I worked with always had nice outfits. I always wore the same ones. I just wanted to be pretty like them and look nice. I excitedly fixed my hair and curled it well.

I went outside and Albert still wasn't back with my car. I knew I was going to be late and that Albert did this on purpose so I couldn't go to work. I started to ask a neighbor if they could take me to work when Albert pulled up. He looked at me and got out of the car with a five-gallon bucket of paint that was filled halfway. He got the water hose and was spraying water into the bucket.

Albert told me right then to go inside and change my clothes and that he didn't like my outfit I had on. I told him, "I just bought this outfit and I like it and I am not changing."

Rage filled his eyes and he started to spray me with the hose. The water was extremely cold, I was shivering and numb when he then threw the hose to the ground and said, "Go change!"

I said, "No, I am not changing and you need to take me to work now! We will discuss my outfit when I get home." He then picked up the bucket and threw the dirty white paint water over my head. He pulled my hair and pulled me down to the ground and told me, "You're not going to work." I took off running and he yelled at me, "I'm not going to chase you, bitch!"

I ran and ran until I got to work and I actually only ended up fifteen minutes late after all that. I was so proud that I made it there and I defied Albert and went anyway. I showed him who was boss, right?

I opened my window and set my money up and my boss called me in the back office for a minute. She said, "Bonnie, what is going on and why do you look like this?"

I told her the truth about what happened and she just looked at me very calmly said, "You are a hard worker and I love you girl; however, you have a lot of personal issues going on in your life right now and need to fix them and then come back when you're ready." This was devastating to hear.

I said, "No, please let me keep my job, this is all I have that I can look forward to and know I matter."

She actually had tears come down her face and said, "I know, and that's what makes this so much harder to do. You need to leave him; he is ruining your life." She told me to look at my face in the mirror. I looked at myself and saw my makeup running down my face and mascara smeared across my right cheek and white, dried up paint in my hair. I had a red, scuffed up nose and my left cheek was bruised and scabbed. There was paint all down the front of my damp clothes. I knew I was a mess. I was a big mess. I was a fucking mess!

I knew this was it; I had reached rock bottom. What in the hell had happened to me and why did I allow myself to be treated like this?

If this wasn't bad enough, I found out I was pregnant again.

I wasn't happy; I thought about an abortion and then knew I didn't have the money to do it. I started thinking, *How am I going to have another baby in this life* and *I'm such a horrible mother not being strong enough to leave my abusive drug addicted husband.*

What am I going to do now? I had no one to go to and was literally all alone.

CHAPTER ELEVEN

Desperate Measures

I was in a lonely, dark world now and angry because my life had become nothing.

How could I allow myself to become such a mess? I was now living behind my mother-in-law in a garage that was converted into a house. I sat alone one night while my son was spending the night with his cousins. I didn't know where Albert was again and I truly didn't care anymore. I just didn't want to live anymore.

I went to sleep that night and cried myself to sleep praying to God to please not let me wake up the next morning. The next morning, of course I woke up and I screamed at God, "How can you let me live like this? Why won't you just let me die in my sleep?"

I went outside and started throwing myself into the garage door as hard as I could. I ran to the end of the driveway and then I ran as fast as I could up to the garage door and threw my stomach and chest into it, hoping to cause a miscarriage.

After I exhausted myself, I ran into the house and shut the door. I looked through all my medicine, wanting to overdose. I only had Tylenol. I then got the sharpest knife I could find and tried to stab myself in the chest but didn't have enough guts.

I then said to myself, "If I kill myself then I win and Albert loses because he didn't kill me. I killed myself first!" I got the knife and started slicing as fast as I could into my wrists and they were starting to open and bleed. They burned. I then said to myself, "I can't do it this way. I'm going to run the car off of the overpass of the 215 freeway and the 10 freeway overpass."

I wrote a suicide note so that my son and everyone would know I loved them and it had nothing to do with them, but only with my unhappiness and no way out.

I had been unhappy for so long that I didn't even know what happiness was anymore.

I knew it was a matter of time before Albert killed me anyway. I truly didn't see any light at the end of the tunnel. I had no life. I hadn't lived for a few years and felt like I had died years before that anyway. I had no friends. And the small family I had didn't know the truth of what I was going through because I hid it from them since I was so ashamed of who I had allowed myself to become.

I knew I was losing it: I was rocking back and forth on my kitchen floor and then would yell at God about forsaking me and not answering my prayers and my desperate pleas for help.

I waited for Albert to come home so I could leave to kill myself, but he never came.

I started to yell at God again, "You don't exist! You don't answer my cries to you!"

I remembered a girl down the street that he was screwing around with, and I found him at her apartment. I barged in her front door and they were making out in the living room. I saw love letters he had written her and flowers on the table by the door. He never bought me flowers. I immediately grabbed the letters so I could read them later, just for my curiosity to see what he had to say to her.

At that very moment, I heard Albert running up behind me, and he started chasing me as I ran back to the house. He shot his gun off in the air and said stop. I told him to go ahead and shoot me, I wanted to die. I told him I am not afraid anymore.

I could tell on his face he knew I wasn't kidding. He saw my wrists and said, "What have you done to yourself?" He found some rags and put them with ice on my wrists.

"Are you fucking stupid?" He asked.

I said, "I am leaving you."

"You are not leaving anywhere," he quickly responded. I ran for the door so I could take off in the car and finish what I had started. He grabbed me and backhanded me so hard across my face, I felt dizzy and fell to the ground. He had hit me so hard in my right ear, it was making a ringing sound and felt hot to the touch. Albert then started banging my head into the ground over and over until he was out of breath. Then he yelled from the top of his lungs, "Why do you make me do this to you?"

I just laid there lifeless; I had no more fight in me. My whole body hurt from throwing myself into the garage and slitting my wrists, which at this point had stopped bleeding. I started to break everything in my living room and threw every knickknack we had. I wanted to throw away every memory we had.

Albert took off in the car and I watched the lights fade out. I was done.

I was still screaming at God as I sat in the middle of all the broken furniture and mess. I was so desperate and angry and screaming at the top of my lungs an agonizing cry that sounded truly like I was dying.

Suddenly I heard a voice in my head that I feel was God answering me.

It was man's voice, deep but loving, and he said to go out the door and do not look back. I said, "Why haven't you helped me?"

He said to me, "My child you need to help yourself first and I will guide you and be with you always. I have heard your cries, but you were not ready to help yourself." I couldn't believe what I was hearing! *Was I losing it? Is this real? Is God talking to me or have I seriously once and for all lost my fucking mind?!*

A couple of hours later, I heard police sirens and I knew it was Albert.

My heart dropped as I listened to them obviously chasing someone.

Sure enough, he had committed some sort of a burglary and they caught him. He was sentenced to two years. I ended up having to go through almost my entire pregnancy alone, but I knew this was what needed to happen.

I was hoping that he could be saved from his own worst enemy: himself.

My life was now about to really begin.

Bonnie, with son Daniel and daughter Nicole

CHAPTER TWELVE

Finding Myself

In August 1995, my daughter was born. I named her Nicole after Nicole Brown Simpson.

She was my angel and looked just like Snow White. I was not able to nurture her the way most moms do, though. I have felt guilty about this her entire life, that I was not there with her during her first couple of years. I was not really there emotionally as I should have been.

I was finding myself; I had started to take police science classes and moved on to graduate from the police academy. This all took a lot of my time.

I quickly was whipped into shape and started to go out with different men as well.

I dated a police officer and had sex with him a few times and a radio show DJ in San Bernardino. However, I really just wanted to settle down and show my kids that there is another side to life that is good. I had sworn off Mexicans, since Albert was Mexican. I intended to find myself a secure white older man.

One night in December of 1996, I went to a restaurant and nightclub called Bobby McGee's in San Bernardino. A nice Mexican guy approached me and told me his name was Art. He asked me my name and if I wanted to dance. My girlfriend who was with me that night told him my name was Barbara. He looked at me and said, "She can't speak for herself?"

I told him, "My name is Bonnie. I do not wish to dance right now but thank you."

He said, "OK, well let me know if you change your mind." He had a perfect smile and smelled really good and was dressed nice. His accent turned me off, though, as I knew he was from Mexico.

Later that night, he was dancing with a really pretty girl and I saw that could dance very well. I will admit I was a tad jealous.

He came up to me again a little bit later and asked me if I would like him to buy me a drink. I politely declined and then the song "California Knows How to Party" came on.

I loved that song and started moving my body to the sound of the music. He took me by my hand and we danced the rest of the night. It wasn't much later that we began speaking on the phone regularly. We would talk for hours and it seemed like just a few minutes. He showed me so much attention and I craved that. I wanted that; hell, I needed that.

I really began to like him.

Later on, he had told me that night when I declined to dance with him, he purposely walked the whole place to find the prettiest girl to dance with so that I would see and be jealous. I do remember him frequently looking at me while he was dancing with her. We laugh about it now, as it was so funny at the time.

Art was very romantic and always made sure I felt special. He bought me two dozen roses on our two month anniversary and a bunch of balloons for Valentine's Day. He treated me better in two months than Albert had in the entire eleven years we were together. Art supported me in my law enforcement career and was a good father to his three children.

I thought I had finally found happiness and normalcy in my life. Was this love? Was this what life is truly all about?

*Bonnie, with her best friend
and husband of 15 years*

CHAPTER THIRTEEN

New Life

Some time had gone by and Albert was now out of prison.

I was hoping that he had learned his lesson in prison and finally changed from doing the drugs. After just a short time, he was back on the drugs again.

I had lived by myself in apartments in Fontana and I was doing very well for myself. I had finally made friends with a few people and my neighbor Lisa became my best friend. I met her at the pool in our apartment. It was funny; she thought I was crazy when she met me because I told her all my stories of Albert's abuse the first day I met her. We are still best friends to this day.

Albert ended up getting custody of the kids every other weekend from 7 p.m. Friday to 6 p.m. on Sunday.

I didn't like this agreement but I wasn't going to keep the kids from their father either. I knew what it was like without my real father in my life and I didn't want to put my kids through that.

One Friday, Albert came to get the kids and he couldn't find my daughter's shoes. I was at Lisa's apartment and told him to go ahead and go in my living room to get her shoe. He found her shoe and they left and all was good.

I thought it was strange because he was nicer this night to me then he usually was. I thought maybe we were moving past things now and could get along civilly for our children.

About two hours later, my phone rang in my living room and I answered it.

It was Albert. His demeanor had changed and he talked in a very low scary voice that I had never heard before.

"You think that you're cool, you fucking bitch. You're nothing but a dead pig. I am going to dress your boyfriend up in a dress and fuck him in the ass, and I'm going to kill you once and for all."

At this point, I could tell that he must have gone and gotten high again. I asked him, "Where are the kids?"

He said, "Don't worry about it." I started to tremble as I worried about if he had done something to them. I had to speak to him calmly and rationally so I could assess the situation.

I said, "Albert, this has to stop already, I don't want to fight anymore. I love you and will always love you, but I cannot save you and I cannot be with you. I am not a possession; I am a human. You have your freedom now, you can do whatever you want, and I am not there to hold you down or question you for that matter. Please let me go on with my life, this is all I ask of you."

Albert replied, "I am on my way to kill you, Bonnie."

I said, "Well you better make sure you do it this time then because I have a gun and I will use it on you if I have to."

He laughed wickedly and said, "That's funny. Do you notice anything missing?"

The hair rose up on the back of my neck. I stretched my phone cord as far as I could to my police closet, and I opened the door, thinking, *Please be there; please don't let him have taken my gun. Oh my God, what am I going to do?*

Suddenly, I heard the phone bang back and forth and I could tell that he was at a corner pay phone.

I quickly hung up once I noticed my entire police gun case gone. I had rounds of magazines in it, my loaded gun, handcuffs, and pepper spray.

I started crying and called 911 to tell them my ex was on his way to kill me.

They had a K-9 unit patrolling the area, and at that very time, I heard the police officers yelling outside my apartment complex to stop and they commanded the police K-9 dogs to attack. Gun shots went off and my gun went flying into the swimming pool.

My law enforcement career was ruined and I thought, *Once again he is never going to let me be or be in peace.*

I will never forget the look in his eyes, the sadness and desperation as he was lying on his stomach handcuffed. He knew then he lost me and his control over me once and for all. That night, I fell on my knees and cried and felt weak because I knew it was finally over.

He ended up getting four years in prison for this and during that time we spoke through letters and he finally promised me he was going to let me go.

He would have killed me that day; I know it in my heart.

Once again he took my identity from me and I needed to find myself.

I can no longer look back at the what ifs and could have beens. I knew I had tried everything I could to make my marriage work. You cannot save someone from themselves. It is also the hardest to forgive someone who hasn't asked for forgiveness.

I forgave him and came to peace within myself. I no longer felt guilty for not being able to change him.

I now needed to move on with my life and again not look back.

I had spoken to my aunt about everything one day and she told me that they always knew everything that was going on for the most part. I asked her, "How come you didn't say anything?"

She told me, "Bonnie, had I said anything against Albert, you would have sided with him because you were so dependent on him. It would have pushed you further away and I would never have known if you were OK or dead if I lost base with you."

I knew she was right. She may not have known exactly how bad my hell was, but she knew enough. This had saddened me and she told me, "I am so proud of you, Bonnie, don't be sad."

Bonnie, Graduation Day from the Police Academy

Bonnie, on her wedding day in 2001, to her best friend Art

CHAPTER FOURTEEN

Moving Forward

Everything I worked hard for with law enforcement had ended for now.

At least I found myself. I did end up going back to college later and obtained a degree in criminology, but it just never really fit back into my life again.

I was a new person now and learned from all of it.

I started working at a truck dealership. Who would have ever thought that this would end up being my lifelong career after all?

I love being able to be my goofy self and help customers to get their trucks back on the road to make money. It is my passion to give the best customer service, whatever way that may be.

On April 7, 2001, I married my best friend Arturo, the man who taught me how to love and trust again.

My aunt passed away suddenly on Thursday, January 27, 2005, the same weekend Art and I moved to Phoenix, Arizona, to transfer with our jobs. This took a toll on me, as I always thought she was the strongest person alive. I learned how precious life was at that point.

My mom ended up having three strokes the following year, which took another toll on me: trying to take care of her and run a family and also work a full time career.

My aunt's girlfriend Pat also passed away in December 2008, and I felt a loss, as it was a realization that everyone I knew and helped raise me was passing away.

In January 2015, my son lost his daughter, Ava Marie, a week before her due date and later found out she had leukemia. She was my first biological granddaughter. I have two step-granddaughters now and they are so beautiful.

I started doing comedy after my friends told me that they thought I should pursue it part time. I am at home on the stage with a microphone in my hand. I just go up there and tell my true life funny events. I love opening for headliners. I have worked with Pete Davidson, who is on *SNL*, and also Lisa Landry.

Without laughter, we only have sadness. We have to be able to laugh to live.

We all have tragedies in our lives; some more than others. Just look forward and know everything is going to be OK.

Bonnie Romero

Learn from your mistakes; pick yourself back up each time you fall. You will eventually get to where you are headed. Just remember that no one takes your power, you have to give it to them.

Trust me that if I could get through what I went through, you can get through whatever situation you are in. There are many resources out there.

If you are in a relationship where you are abused, whether it be physical or mental, you need to get out of it. That person does not love you. It is about control.

I had to share my story and also my imperfections so that hopefully I can help some man or woman to know that violence is not OK. You are beautiful and you matter.

There is someone out there for every one of us, and if you just focus on you, that person will eventually come along when you at least expect it. Be true and do what is right and the rest will fall into place.

You can reach me on my website if you need resources: BeBonafied.com.

Look for my show dates to be announced on my website, or you can purchase copies of my book.

Live, love, and laugh!

Bonnie Romero
Author

www.ingramcontent.com/pod-product-compliance
Lightning Source LLC
Chambersburg PA
CBHW071534080526
44588CB00011B/1671